Critical Connection
A Practical Guide to Parenting Young Teens

WORKBOOK

ANDY KERCKHOFF

Andy Kerckhoff is a middle school teacher and the author of the blog *Growing Up Well*. He and his wife have been married for twenty years and have two teenage children.

Kerckhoff has served in various educational roles for over twenty years, including as an elementary school principal in Whitefish, Montana, and a high school teacher in Dallas, Texas. He currently serves as a seventh-grade English and World Geography teacher at Westminster Christian Academy in Saint Louis, Missouri.

White Orchard Press
Critical Connection: A Practical Guide for Parenting Young Teens - Workbook
Andy Kerckhoff

Cover Design: Andrew Kristyan
Formatter: Nicole Hutchins

Published in the United States by White Orchard Press
ISBN :9780991131815

Version 1.0
Printed by CreateSpace, a DBA of On-Demand Publishing, LLC

INTRODUCTION

Since the release of *Critical Connection*, a number of people have requested a workbook. It is only natural that some parents who are already in a book club, dinner group, or church small group would want to discuss in depth some of the parenting issues raised in the book. Others might just want to dig deeper into their own personal analysis.

This workbook is designed, like its companion book, to be highly practical, thought provoking, and easy to use and re-use. It is organized topically; therefore, a group can easily pick which topics they want to read and discuss, cafeteria style.

This workbook is to be used any way the user wishes. There is no system. It's a resource. Feel free to do whatever seems best. Here are a few options:
- just think about the questions without writing anything
- pick only a few questions to explore in long written responses
- discuss every question in a chapter over several small group meetings

Quotes from the original book are in bold italics and have the page numbers in parentheses. If you own the book, I recommend reading each chapter before answering the questions. This will yield the best results.

I sincerely hope that these questions provoke deep introspection, conversation, and application in the life of your family.

For further articles, links, and videos related to raising young teens, follow me on Twitter at GrowingUpWell and subscribe to my blog GrowingUpWell.org.

CONTENTS

PART 1 - CONNECTIONS

BE THE PARENT

"I don't believe there is a formula for success when it comes to raising healthy and happy children, but there are good practices and bad practices. There are things that generally work and things that generally do not." **(3) (from page 3 in the paperback of** *Critical Connection***)**

1. Who are the best parents you know? List several, if you can.

2. What makes them good parents? Be specific.

3. Who is your parenting role model?

4. Of the four parent traps, which one do you tend to be?

   Friend   Judge   Uncle   Helicopter

5. What types were your own parents?

"Simply put, avoid the extremes. Do not be the most permissive, most cool, most involved, most strict, or most anything parent." **(7)**

6. Do you tend to lean toward an extreme? If so, describe what your extremism can look like.

"The best parents are the ones who care enough to say, 'No, you can't do that, because I love you too much to let you settle for that kind of life.'(7) Be the one who calls the shots, sets the agenda, and makes the tough choices." **(8)**

7. Do you struggle with being the authority? When do your kids run the show?

8. What are some obstacles to managing your family well?

9. Are you willing to acknowledge your weaknesses as a parent? If so, there is great hope! What are some of your soft spots as a parent?

Takeaway - Every parent has blind spots and weak spots. Know thyself.

Actions Steps: I will...

THE EARLY YEARS

"It was especially hard for me from ten to fourteen... Fortunately, I had some powerful healing agents?" (11)

1. Describe what was difficult about your life when you were a young teen.

2. Do you have any scars from your early life that may be affecting your parenting?

3. What were your healing agents?

4. Who were the most influential people in your life when you were a young teen?

5. What was the best thing that your parents and/or caregivers did for you?

6. Do you agree that "*our kids will not do a good job of raising themselves*"?

Takeaway: Your children need healing agents in their lives.

Actions Steps: I will...

FAMILIES MATTER

"One family lives with each other, while the other is on the run, often in opposite directions... One family is a team, while the other is a bunch of individuals, free from the inconveniences of too much family time." (18)

1. Being on the run in opposite directions is inevitable but not desirable. How often is this a problem in your family? Once a week? Once a day? All day every day?

2. Would the people who know your family describe it as a team? How would they describe it?

3. Do your children see themselves as integral members of a team, or do they see themselves as individuals whose family just gets in the way of their personal goals?

"Family identity, like team spirit, is no accident." (20)

4. What is the identity of your team? What is your family known for?

5. If you were to "brand" your team the way a marketer brands a company, what are some slogan ideas?

"It takes a village to raise a young man or woman well, but it all starts in the home with a team approach." (21)

6. Brainstorm some ideas about how you can create more bonding in your family.

7. If you were to make a family crest, what are some symbols you might use?

8. If your children had to write a paper for school describing their family, what might you expect to read?

Takeaway: Create family bonds and a family identity.

Actions Steps: I will...

DEFINING ADOLESCENCE

"If there is just one way to describe middle school students, it is **dynamic.** *Nothing stays the same in the life of a middle school kid." (23)*

1. How do you tend to react to the dynamic nature of young teens? Does it excite you or terrify you?

2. How well do you think you understand this stage of life called early adolescence?

"Making a connection is the first step toward influencing young teenagers." (24)

3. Do you see yourself as a leader? Who follows you?

4. How well do you feel that you understand where your young teen is right now, as opposed to last year?

"In order to connect with early adolescents, it is important to understand them to some degree. We must have appropriate expectations of what they are -- not children anymore, but not fully adult yet, either." (25)

5. Define early adolescence in your own words.

6. What are the characteristics of maturity that you want your children to have by the time they are eighteen?

7. Circle the characteristics in the above list that are non-negotiables.

8. These non-negotiables should be in a family mission statement or family crest or something important. Consider where theses values belong. They should be posted prominently somewhere in your home.

"Maturing is a long process. It's crockpot cooking." (28)

9. Do you understand that maturing is a messy, lengthy process? Is this a new idea to you? If so, does that change anything about the way you parent?

10. Now that you have some long-term goals for your children's character (see above), what is the timeline for achieving those goals?

From the "Top Ten Things You Should Know About Your Middle School Student" by Steve Hall:
"Each middle school student has one compelling mission each day: Avoid embarrassment!" (28)

11. Does this explain any of your young teen's behavior? Give an example.

"Their thinking is characterized by over-analysis and is often followed by a definitive black-and-white conclusion to the matter... Abstract thinking is emerging at this age, but oftentimes in an awkward way." (30)

12. How does this affect your conversations?

13. How do you typically react to this sort of "debate?"

"A middle school child's problems don't always seem big to us, because our age and experience allow us to live in a bigger world." (31)

14. Do you often find yourself rolling your eyes at the petty nature of your child's "major problems?"

15. How can you better react to your child's big-problem-in-a-very-small-world freakout?

"Adolescence is a stage many people miss out on because they are either looking back at the cute elementary school years or forward to the more glamorous high school years." (32)

16. Do you have a positive attitude about adolescence or do your see it as something to just survive?

Takeaway: Adolescence is a slow process of learning and growing in maturity. Lead with understanding.

Actions Steps: I will...

"You cannot go wrong with giving your children honest affirmation at home." (36)

1. In the area of daily affirmation of your children, what are your tendencies at home? How do you do it? How often? How is it received? How would your spouse or relatives describe you in this regard?

2. Which of the following affirmations are strengths of yours and which are weaknesses?

   Constructive Words
   Asking Questions
   Caring Touch
   Shared Experiences
   Meaningful Gifts

3. Which of these are most meaningful to each of your children?

4. Do your strengths match up with your kids' needs?

"Mundane situations like riding in a car or watching TV provide countless opportunities for expressing your pleasure and pride in your child with constructive words." (37)

5. How often does the whole family sit around the table for a meal?

6. What are mealtimes like in your home? Is bonding happening?

7. If you are not good at caring touch, what are some safe ways that you can make contact?

8. What sorts of shared activities work well for the whole family?

9. What shared activities are the most special for each child?

10. What sorts of gifts, big or small, are most appreciated by each member of your family?

Takeaway: Young teens need affirmation more than ever. Strive every day to express your love more effectively.

Actions Steps: I will...

TAKING CARE OF YOURSELF

"Every active, conscientious parent needs to know how to practice sustainable parenting." (47)

1. Do you feel that you can sustain your style of parenting for as long as your kids are in your home under your care?

"Parents who expect too much of themselves face even graver consequences: parents who break down will neglect or hurt their kids, one way or another." (48)

2. Do you ever feel like you are going to have a breakdown?

3. What are the factors that send you to the edge of physical and/or mental health?

4. Which of those factors are things that you can control?

5. What keeps you from making lifestyle changes to help reduce the frequency and intensity of breakdowns?

"Set realistic expectations. Perfection is not the goal of family life." (50)

6. Do you struggle with perfectionism? Does your spouse? Is this a source of conflict in your home?

7. What are some unrealistic expectations that your have in your family life? (Time, money, relationships)

8. Which area -- time, money, or relationships -- is the most difficult for you to set realistic expectations?

"Materialism makes us miserable. It is the silent enemy of contentment. We can combat it." (51)

9. Where is your biggest weakness in your battle against materialism?

10. What are some small ways that you can combat materialism in your life?

"Balance is a myth. The people who accomplish great things are not as well balanced as you would think. You can't have it all or do it all, no matter how hard you try." (53)

11. Do you strive for balance and perfection daily?

12. Do you think you could let go of the idea of balancing everything? What would be the result?

"Practice thanksgiving. Tally up the 95% of your life that is going well and being taken for granted." (54)

13. How often do you practice giving thanks? What daily rituals of thanks can you implement?

Takeaway: Parents must take care of themselves enough to sustain parenthood over the long haul. Setting realistic expectations and practicing thanksgiving are fundamental in the pursuit of happiness.

Actions Steps: I will...

FEAR LESS

"Fears permeate our personal lives and are diffused into our family lives." (58)

1. What were some of your parents' biggest fears?

2. What are some of your biggest fears as a parent?

3. Which of those are legitimate it-could-happen-to-you-someday fears?

4. Which ones are totally irrational never-going-to-happen fears?

5. Which fears are on the edge of Crazytown but are not totally irrational?

6. Do some of your fears inhibit your children from some great experiences? Ask your spouse or someone who knows you really well.

"Train your child to be smart, have fun, and wear a helmet when riding his bike. Just don't let fear rule the day. It's more dangerous for kids to sit inside eating junk food and playing video games -- even though it's less scary." (63)

7. What are some ways that you can encourage your kids to have fun in slightly dangerous activities?

8. Did that question make your uncomfortable? Why (or why not)?

9. What are the risks of a safe and sedentary lifestyle?

"Independence is the goal." *(64)*

10. Where does instilling independence fall in your list of primary goals as a parent?

11. Give an example from the last week of something you have done to foster independence in your child.

12. Why is it difficult for parents to push their kids toward independence?

13. How does fostering independence in the child reduce fear in the parent?

"Rules without relationship leads to rebellion." *(66)*

14. How does strengthening the parent-child bond reduce fear in the parent?

Takeaway - Reduce your parenting fears by reasoning with yourself, strengthening relationships, and fostering independence in your children.

Actions Steps: I will...

PART 2 – GUIDANCE

THE HEART MATTERS MOST

"Parenting well has an order of operations. Insides come first." (73)

1. How would you describe the quality of and characteristics of your emotional relationships with your children?

"If a child thinks you might give up on them, he will probably give up first." (74)

2. Do you think that your children truly, deeply believe that you will never give up on them, no matter what they do or say? How do you know? How might you determine that?

"Trouble comes when parents react to symptoms rather than causes. Behavior is a reflection of an inner reality." (75)

3. Were you raised by parents who were behavior managers, or were they interested in nourishing a solid relationship first and foremost?

4. How do you parent? Honestly, are you a behavior manager?

5. What could you do (or not do) this week to show your children that you don't care about their outer behavior as much as you care about their inner life?

"Boundaries are meant to protect kids and to train them to someday be self-disciplined." (76)

6. Do your children understand the above statement? How do you know?

7. Is self-management one of your parenting goals?

8. Do you communicate to your kids that you expect them to increase in self-control so that one day you will not have to guide them anymore? Do they know that you want them to be on their own one day?

"Author Jon Carroll wrote, 'Success is boring. Success is proving that you can do something that you already know you can do. Failure is how we learn." (77)

9. What is your attitude toward making mistakes? Does making a mistake create anxiety in your own life? Does it deeply disturb you, or do you tend to roll with the punches and not sweat mistakes?

10. Do other family members struggle with perfectionism and anxiety over failure?

11. Is your family culture one that embraces mistakes as learning moments or is failure generally unacceptable?

12. How do your kids view failure? How do they respond to mistakes?

13. Do your kids have the attitude that they can do poorly at something at first, and it's ok because they know that with practice, they can achieve something worthwhile? Or would they rather not try something new because failure is likely?

"Don't forget the fun. Kids bond with people who make them smile and laugh. You don't have to be all that funny or crazy, as long as you will share what makes you laugh. Sharing a laugh is a force multiplier in the war for a child's heart." (77)

14. What are the fun things you do as a family on a weekly basis?

15. What are your best memories of the past few years?

16. What are your kids' best memories of the past few years?

17. Do you need to schedule some fun events that will make great lifelong memories?

18. Do you need to inject some fun into your daily (or evening) schedule?

Takeaway: Get connected and stay connected with your kids with unconditional love, a healthy response to mistakes, and lots of fun.

Actions Steps: I will...

DISCIPLINE

"Parents must be far more than legislators, law-enforcement officers, and judges." (80)

1. What is the difference between punishment and discipline?

2. What is the goal of loving discipline?

3. What are the character traits of a good disciplinarian?

4. Do you tend toward justice or mercy as a disciplinarian? Are you the good cop or bad cop?

5. Who do you know that most effectively disciplines children? Who do you know who personifies loving discipline of young teens? (parent, teacher, coach, counselor...)

6. Why do you think only the extremes (too lax or too tough) get all the attention?

"Being in control as a parent is very different than being controlling. Being in control is positive. It is firm and purposeful. It is intentional. Being controlling is negative. It is manipulative. It employs cheap tricks like guilt." (83)

7. What are some cheap tricks that your parents used on you to control you?

8. What are some cheap tricks that you have used in the past to control your children?

9. What are some specific ways that you can get yourself in control when you need it most, when your child is out of control?

"You have to downshift. Decelerate the conflict." (86)

10. What are some things you can do and say to decelerate a conflict with your child?

11. When arguments flare, who is in control in your house? Anyone?

12. When you lose control and blow it, how do your get it back? Do you ever apologize in order to gain control?

"Negotiation is a vital life skill, and parents need to teach children how to do it well." (87)

13. How are you at negotiating with your kids? Is negotiation a nightmare, or is it usually a civil discourse?

14. Do your kids understand that no means no? Or do they balk at every no?

15. Do you and your kids have a way of talking, listening, and reconsidering things, without being in a win-lose situation?

Takeaway: Disciplining young teens is about training them for adulthood. It's not about controlling them. It's a process of intentionally teaching them valuable lessons in a loving way.

Actions Steps: I will...

RESILIENCE

"Life is extraordinarily unfair. Dare we tell our kids the truth?" (91)

1. Do your kids know that life is unfair?

2. How do you usually respond to their pleas of "It's not fair!"

3. Do your kids demand that you fix everything for them that is broken or unfair?

4. Do you tend to rescue your kids from every injustice and trouble?

5. Would you rather fix a problem or explain a problem to your children?

"The good news of an unfair life is that life is hard but God is good -- all the time. Kids deserve to know this because it will help them process injustice better. The sooner they realize this, the better." (93)

6. When do you think it is appropriate to explain the unfairness of life to your children? What is a good age to have those deep, difficult discussions?

7. Does your family understand that they are unfairly blessed in many ways? Do you have those discussions?

"No parent or teacher would prescribe it, but the truth is that pain is necessary. Suffering is the prerequisite for service, compassion, love, and a host of other first-rate character traits." (94)

8. Is it difficult for you to have pain in your own life and embrace it as a sign of growth and development?

9. How comfortable are you with growing pains in your children?

10. Do you convey that all pain is bad?

"Anything worth doing well is worth doing poorly at first." (98)

11. How well do your kids bounce back from failure?

"Resilience is the capacity to recover from adversity and return to well-being." (99)

12. Are your kids growing in resilience, or are they paralyzed with the fear of failure?

13. Are your kids learning to be tough in the right way, exhibiting kind strength?

14. Do they at least have that vision that adults should be both loving and strong?

15. What are some ways that you can teach "kind strength" to kids? (role models, martial arts, books...)

Takeaway: *"Equipping our children for independence requires us to guide them, not rescue them, as they handle adversity." (100)*

Actions Steps: I will...

SOCIALIZATION

"Our kids are growing up in this isolating world, and it is up to us -- the adults who they rely upon -- to teach them how to engage with communities." (102)

1. What are some aspects of modern American culture that isolate people?

2. Are any of those things problematic for you?

3. Which of those things do you think could be a problem for your kids?

"Interdependence is just as important as independence." (102)

4. Do you tend to be independent or interdependent or both?

5. In your family culture, which is valued higher? Why?

6. What do you communicate to your kids about independence and interdependence?

"If we join communities, integrate our kids into them, give them a purpose within them, and let them enjoy the benefits, our kids will grow up more able to relate to a variety of people in a variety of settings." (103)

7. List the communities to which you belong.

8. Which of your communities are the most important and deserve top priority?

9. Which of your communities are less important to you and deserve lower priority?

"As parents, we make choices (or we let others choose for us) about what academic, athletic, and artistic institutions our children will be in, and that greatly affects their development." (104)

10. List all the institutions that your children belong to.

11. Which of these are the most valuable to your children and your family?

12. Which ones are the less valuable to you?

"Schools are not one-size-fit-all. Sometimes it's necessary to reconsider school choices each year for each child." (105) "I also think it's important to regularly reconsider teams and other groups that they're involved in." (106)

13. Are there any institutions in your life that are not really helping your children grow up well?

14. Are there any changes that your family should consider?

"One of the most important things I can do for my children is to them with other adults who will act as role models in ways that I cannot." (106)

15. Who are the best role models for your children?

16. Is there anything you can do to support them?

17. Are there any other people you know who would be superb role models? Is there a way to connect your kids with them?

"Kids with good manners will stand out as all-stars." (109)

18. How would you rate your children's social skills for their age?

19. Are there any weaknesses in social skills that you think they should work on? Remember, it's a work in progress.

20. What should they work on right now?

Takeaway: Our kids need social circles, role models, and social skills. Put them in the best places for them to get the kind of socialization you prefer. Be intentional about it.

Actions Steps: I will...

SOCIAL LIFE

"It actually just takes a few good friends in a few key places to have a meaningful social life." (111)

1. Name each of your kids' best friends.

2. Does each of your children have at least one good, solid friendship?

3. Do your kids' friends know you? Do you talk with them?

"It is more important for a kid to learn how to make friends than to sit at the cool table at lunch." (111)

4. Do your kids worry about being "popular" to an unhealthy degree?

5. How can you help your kids deal with the cool kids and their cliques?

"Boys need to share certain kinds of experiences in order to make friends... physical... silly... risk-taking... adventurous... playful experiences." (113)

6. Does your boy have access to masculine experiences that are physical, silly, risky, and adventurous?

7. Does your boy have friends with whom to share those experiences?

8. Does your boy move enough everyday? What are his physical activities?

"Boys should treat girls differently than they treat each other. There needs to be a much higher level of care and respect." (114)

9. Does your boy treat girls with a high degree of respect and care?

"Girls should not put up with abuse. Instead, they should be empowered to get help. It needs to be dealt with." (116)

10. Does your girl have the social skills and confidence to stand up for herself?

11. Does your girl have meaningful relationships with a variety of other girls? Who are they?

12. Does your girl have unconditional, loving relationships with her family members?

"Just say no to middle school dating. In my experience, there is no benefit and plenty of detriment at this early stage of development. Focus on making friends and developing a strong sense of self." (116)

13. When do you think it is optimal for a young person to begin dating?

14. When do you think you would allow your young teen to start dating?

15. What would you say to your young teen if you decided to forbid a budding romance?

"Every child, especially the young teen, needs to develop a healthy sense of self, and that cannot happen when a parent is constantly comparing him or her to a sibling, a neighbor, or a peer at school. Comparison is a trap. Avoid it." (119)

16. Do any of your children perceive favoritism in your family? Why?

17. Although you may not say it out loud, do you find yourself making certain comparisons among your kids? Are any of them fair comparisons? Is there such a thing as a fair comparison?

18. Do your kids have a sense of self yet?

19. What is your biggest concern about each child's social life?

20. Have you explained to your children how to make friends?

Takeaway: Young teens need a social life beyond the family. Do what you can to foster your children's friendships.

Actions Steps: I will...

CAREER

"Our kids need less sugarcoated fantasy and more wise guidance toward real-world success." (122)

1. Do your kids hope to play professional sports, perform in entertainment, or have other celebrity dreams?

2. Do you have any dreams for your kids that are fantastic (fame & fortune)?

"For millions of kids, anything less than stardom is a shattered dream, and they do not have a plan B for their future." (122)

3. Have you had any discussions with your children about how rare it is to gain fame in sports or entertainment?

4. Do your kids have any plan B career options that they are considering?

"Kids can explore real-world applications of their talents and interest, but that takes adult guidance." (123)

5. What are your kids' talents and interests?

6. What general career paths might possibly fit with each of your children?

"Be honest about what you see in your kids, but choose your words carefully. They matter." (124)

7. Have you had conversations with your children and other family members about career paths for your kids? Are there any common themes in those conversations?

"Many of our kids have disabilities, and it is essential to focus on their abilities, rather than hyper-focusing on their inabilities. Our job is to guide them toward success in their areas of strength." (124)

8. Are your children each aware of their academic strengths and other skills?

9. Do they have opportunities in and out of school to exercise those gifts and talents?

"Wouldn't it be so much more productive to envision a career path at the age of sixteen, instead of twenty? Our kids will only benefit from early guidance if it is an honest running dialogue and is not overly prescriptive." (127)

10. When do you think it is necessary for a young person to decide on a general career path? When is too early and when is too late to know?

Takeaway: Know your children's academic strengths, skills, and interests, so that you can discuss careers with them and help them narrow their focus toward a successful, satisfying occupation.

Action Steps: I will...

EDUCATION

"At best, we teach our children more than knowledge, more than wisdom. We teach them to love learning."
(132)

1. Do your kids enjoy learning at school?

2. Where do they enjoy learning the most? Where do they thrive as a learner?

2. What types of learning do they enjoy most? What sorts of learning activities do you have to tear them away from?

3. Are they a certain type of learner? (hands on, reader, movement, visual, social, music...)

"When we show interest in their developing opinions and their mental gymnastics, we affirm them deep down and encourage their intellectual growth and independence. Listening is the key." (132)

4. How do you know what your kids are learning?

5. How would you rate yourself as a listener to what your kids are learning?

The following is a brief summary of the "20 Tips That Will Help Your Child Succeed in School" (133-137).

   1. Consider all your school options each year.
   2. Communicate with teachers to establish a relationship.
   3. Consider supplementary school courses.
   4. Limit extracurricular activities to two of the five school nights.
   5. Create a workspace at home.
   6. Set a study time.
   7. Discourage multitasking.
   8. Sit near your child as they work.
   9. Choose a good study partner.
   10. Try a tutor.
   11. Celebrate progress and effort.
   12. Help your child keep a calendar.
   13. Keep backpacks, binders, and lockers organized.

14. Use the school's online gradebook to track progress.
15. Encourage reading for fun.
16. Get your kids to bed early.
17. Treat food and water as a school supply.
18. Eat dinner together.
19. Hug your kids and leave them notes, emails, and text messages.
20. Pray for their academic progress.

6. Of all the things on the above list, what are some areas that you think need improvement?

7. If you could do just one thing better for each of your kids on the above list, what would it be?

"Be careful not to expect too much, push too hard, and suck all the joy and life out of learning." (138)

8. Are you guilty of pushing too hard? Or are you the opposite?

"We have to model learning for our kids. They must see us learning how to do new things." (140)

9. What sorts of things do you love to learn?

10. What are some examples of things you have been learning in the last five years that your kids have observed?

11. Are there commonalities among members of your family regarding learning? Are there any alliances you could make to maximize the things they have in common?

Takeaway: As a parent, you are the primary educator, and your kids need you to help them to love learning and to succeed in school.

Action Steps: I will...

ATHLETICS

"Youth sports, at their best, can instill noble character traits that are extremely useful at school, in relationships, and in careers. But sports must be taken in moderation, balanced with other good things." (142)

1. What are the characteristics that you want your children to learn from participating in sports?

2. What are the other good things that you want to balance with sports?

"Unfortunately, the unintended consequence of a sold-out pursuit of athletic success is a young person who is ultracompetitive, overscheduled, and hyperstressed. Burnout is common." (142)

3. Have you experienced sports burnout in any way as a parent?

4. What are some ways that you can tell if sports are consuming your children or family life?

"Stephen Durant, in his book Whose Game Is It, Anyway? *focuses on three main points: character development, skill development, and age-appropriate expectations. All three are in contrast with what he calls "scoreboard outcomes." (143)*

5. Does anyone in your family prioritize scoreboard outcomes too highly?

6. What does Durant mean when he says to focus on *age-appropriate expectations*?

"Whose game is it anyway? And why are we playing?" (143)

7. Why are each of your kids playing each sport? (i.e. Why is Tommy playing baseball? Why is Jane swimming?)

8. Exactly what do you want from youth sports?

"Praise character when it is good, and correct it when it is bad." (145)

9. Give an example of an effective way to praise your child for good sportsmanship.

10. Give an example of an effective way to correct your child for bad sportsmanship.

"Point out role models. Talk about which players exhibit the best characteristics." (145)

11. Who are some players and coaches that you love? (any sport, any level)

12. Explain exactly why you love them.

"Give kids opportunities to do new things that stretch them. Just be careful not to overschedule them." (145)

13. What activities come easily and are familiar to your children?

14. Can you think of an activity or hobby that would stretch your child without causing overscheduling? (chess, fishing, martial arts...)

"They must not be allowed to lean too heavily on the crutches of athletic talent because those crutches only last so long. Well-rounded kids can handle what life throws at them long after athleticism becomes irrelevant." (146)

15. Would you rather have a well-rounded student athlete or a single-sport all star? Why?

16. Do you have some dreams that you want your kids to fulfill?

17. Whose game is it anyway?

"Play the game for the game's sake." (148)

18. What sports do your kids love so much that they play on their own? What's their passion?

"'How do you think you played?' is a good discussion starter after a game. Remember to focus on effort, character, and the love of the game, rather than scoreboard outcomes." (149)

19. How often do you ask, "Did you win?" or "Did you score?" Is that a hard habit to break?

20. Does anyone in your family tend to focus on scoreboard outcomes? Who?

Takeaway: Strive for a healthy balance in your family's sports participation and seek to keep it fun and full of life lessons, rather than scoreboard outcomes.

Actions Steps: I will...

LOOKING GOOD

"Focus on the inner life first and foremost: the inner person matters most." (154)

"The most important part of helping your child navigate the dangerous waters of self-esteem and body image is conveying that you love them as is. Kids need to know that their parents and other adults love them just the way they are, and that image is not a factor in that love. They must feel secure in their own family and in their own skin." (155)

1. Skin, hair, clothes, and weight are each discussed at length in the book because they are significant areas of conflict among young teens. They often suck up a tremendous amount of time, money, and energy. How would you gauge your child's feelings about each of those categories?

Skin / Makeup

Hair

Clothes

Weight / Shape

2. Is there an area that deserves attention, perhaps a doctor's visit, because it is a serious issue of negligence?

3. Is there an area that is getting too much attention?

4. Do you give too much attention to any of the categories listed above?

"We adults need to be the voice of reason, the ones who eat in moderation, exercise for health's sake, and are not obsessed with our weight or body image." (158)

5. Do you talk a lot about your weight or other physical qualities or fashion? Is image important to you?

"Actions must be paired with the right words. We should not say skinny or fat at all, since those are such loaded words in our culture. We should say things like 'You are looking really healthy' instead of 'You look so skinny in those jeans, and I love what you're doing with your hair.'" (159)

6. How can you encourage the pursuit of health instead of image in your family?

"Image is everything on Instagram and other social media sites." (160)

7. Is your girl's online life filled with cute selfies and fashion pics?

8. Is your boy's online life filled with cool pics promoting his favorite image?

9. Discuss with them what image they are trying to portray online and how they are doing it.

Takeaway: Youth culture is image obsessed, so parents must combat that with every possible angle to teach kids that they can be confident in themselves because they have character and inner beauty.

Actions Steps: I will...

THE NEW MEDIA

"Young people live in a multisensory world of electronica." (164)

1. Do you feel like a native or a tourist in the electronic world?

Types of parental attitudes toward kids' technology: (161-3)
Hands Off = unwilling and unmotivated to learn and help their kids with their tech
Hands Tied = informed, but willing to learn and help
Hands Open = uninformed, but willing to learn and help
Hands Full = able and willing to learn and help

2. Of the four types, which one are you?

3. How about the other adults in your family?

4. What is the biggest obstacle to you becoming a "hands full" parent?

5. Who else in your family can be a helpful guide to your kids' digital lives?

"Teens are far more prone to addictive behavior, and their brains record those good feeling intensely and permanently. A teen who is addicted to something will feel that pull toward that particular addiction throughout his or her life." (164)

6. Are your kids "children of the screen?"

"To the plugged-in young mind, quietness and stillness, two things that religions cherish as spiritual necessities, are awkward and miserable." (165)

7. How are your kids with silence and stillness without devices? Are they comfortable with it?

8. When do your kids get peace and quiet?

9. Do you think that your kids are living in a busy, noisy, always-stimulating world?

"For a whole generation of kids, direct experiences in the backyard, in the tool shed, in the fields and woods, have been replaced by indirect learning, through machines." - Richard Louv (165)

10. Are your kids getting a lot of non-screen experiences?

11. How would they react to a week without screens?

12. Are they addicted to any form of electronics?

"Less is better, in general, but with proper guidance and boundaries, television can be a good teacher." (168)

13. What are the boundaries you have at home regarding the new media (screens)?

14. What are some tips from (or for) other parents? What has helped you the most?

15. What are the best TV shows and movies that you have seen recently?

"Video games are entirely convenient and completely controllable, unlike real life experiences, such as pursuing a new friend, reading a book, or going fishing." (169)

16. Are you concerned about video game addiction in your home?

17. Are you comfortable with the content of the video games in your home?

18. What are some ways that parents can help kids enjoy healthy video games in moderation?

20. How can you go about setting up and enforcing good boundaries without losing your relationship with your children?

Takeaway: *"Get your kids involved with people and physical activities so they are moving, playing, and being creative. It's not enough to say no to screens. Say yes to the other things that make life an adventure."* *(173)*

Action Steps: I will...

MOBILE DEVICES

"I don't think it's a good idea to give a ten- to fourteen-year-old a smartphone." (178)

1. Why is a smartphone a completely different thing than a standard cellphone?

2. Why is the internet browser the real trouble with a smartphone?

3. Do you know how to disable the internet on a mobile device?

4. When do you think you will be ready to setup and monitor a smartphone for your child?

5. When do you think your child will be ready to handle the responsibilities of a smartphone?

"Parents and teachers must be involved in the digital lives of kids. The kids will not find the right path on their own, that is for certain." (179)

6. Are you in the digital world enough to understand what your kids are (or will be) dealing with?

7. Do you think your child is capable of making a big mistake with a mobile device?

"Teach kids to be extremely careful with what they put online, especially on any sort of social media. Every word and image made with a digital device should be assumed to be instantly public and permanent." (182)

8. Does your child understand that their digital lives are not private? Do they understand the "public and permanent" concept?

9. How careful are you and your kids about what you put online?

"One piece of gossip or just one lie can cause a firestorm of online social drama. We cannot just blow it off with a boys-will-be-boys attitude. Cyberbullying should be reported to authorities." (182)

10. Have you or your kids been bullied electronically?

11. Have you spoken with your kids about what they should do if they are cyberbullied?

"Delay all social media involvement as long as possible. I recommend not allowing any social media involvement until a child is fourteen. At that point, ease them in slowly." (182)

12. What are the positive aspects of social media?

13. What are the negative aspects?

"Granting children total online privacy is a very bad idea. Parents should have full access to every account, password, and friendship that kids have on every social media site." (183)

14. What will you say to your kids when they balk at your request to see their devices?

15. Will you have the fortitude to battle over their idea vs. your idea of privacy?

"Set a time, perhaps 8PM, when all devices are turned off and returned to the family docking station in the kitchen or parents' bedroom." (184)

16. Why is it so important to keep mobile devices in public spaces?

"Have a digital sabbath now and then, when the whole family turns off all devices for a day." (184)

17. Have you ever tried a digital sabbath? How did it go? What would you do differently?

18. When in the next two weeks, can you schedule a digital sabbath?

"Do not ever be afraid to tell a young person to put a device away. They need to be taught not to choose screens over people's faces and voices." (185)

19. Do your kids understand why it can be so rude to look at screens at certain times?

20. How good are your own digital manners? What is your weakness?

"It can be helpful to rely on a Family Media Agreement for guidance." (185)

21. What do you think about the idea of discussing and signing an FMA?

Takeaway: Digital citizenship requires parental guidance. Get in the game. Be the coach.

Action Steps: I will...

"Stress reduction, greater physical health, a deeper sense of spirit, more creativity, a sense of play, even a safer life -- these are the rewards that await a family when it invites more nature into children's lives." - Richard Louv (191)

1. What are some of the benefits that nature offers to your family?

2. What is your favorite touchpoint with nature? Where do you get your nature cup filled?

"Kids spend well over forty hours per week in front of electronic screens, but less than forty minutes per week in nature." (192)

3. Are your kids on the NDD spectrum (Nature Deficit Disorder)?

4. What percentage of their life is spent indoors?

5. What percentage of your life is spent indoors?

"The push button culture is working against kids. They are constantly given immediate, customized, positive feedback from their cell phones, tablets, video games, and the Internet. But in real life, and especially in the natural world, there are no fast-forward or reset buttons." (192)

6. What are each of your children's favorite push-button activities?

7. Do you think your kids are negatively affected by the immediate gratification of the push-button digital world?

"Whatever shape nature takes, it offers each child an older, larger world separate from parents. Nature offers healing for a child." (193)

8. What are some of the shapes that nature takes in your family life? Where do you touch nature? (pets, lake, garden...)

9. Do you have a child who seems calmer and happier in nature?

"A fourth grader in San Diego said, "I like to play indoors 'cause that's where all the electric outlets are." (193)

10. What are some ways that you can move some of your family activities outdoors?

"Buy equipment that promotes outdoor play." (195)

11. Are there any things you can buy, such as a hammock or canoe or bicycle, that will get your kids outdoors more often?

12. Could you create a backyard budget to turn your backyard into a play-land and rest-land?

Takeaway: "Let the children play outdoors! Leave no child inside!" (193)

Action Steps: I will...

WORK AND MONEY

"As kids develop, we can slowly reduce the protection and provision while we increase the preparation. In the middle school years, our kids can learn to do adult tasks." (202)

1. What are some adult tasks that your children can learn in the next month?

"They should know that their work is important and that a job well done is greatly valued and that shoddy or incomplete work is a problem for others. Give kids tasks around the house that are age-appropriate and legitimately helpful to others."(203)

2. What are your kids doing for chores these days?

3. Are these chores valuable to the family? Do the kids sense this?

4. What do you think is the best system of allowance?

"We can teach kids that service is not an event. It is a lifestyle. Service is a part of being a family." (203)

6. What daily rituals or chores do you have at home that requires kids to serve others?

"Parents do not intend to spoil their children. It happens naturally, and our culture encourages it." (206)

7. Did your parents spoil you in any way?

8. How do you think the way your parents treated you financially is affecting the way you are raising your own kids financially?

9. In what ways have you spoiled your kids unknowingly in the past?

10. What are some intentional things you can do to keep your kids from being spoiled?

"Personal Finance 101: Earn well. Spend carefully. Give generously. Save wisely." (209)

11. Of the four personal finance topics, which ones do you personally struggle with?

12. How do your kids earn money?

13. Can you think of any other ways that they can earn money with their own labor?

14. Do you require your kids to give money to those in need?

15. Do you require them to save any money?

16. What do they buy for themselves?

17. Describe your kids' attitudes toward money.

18. Describe your kids' attitudes toward work.

Takeaway: Teaching and training children to be financially healthy is a long process, but it is an investment that will bless them and many others for a lifetime.

Action Steps: I will...

FINAL ASSIGNMENT

- Go back and highlight all the action steps that you have determined to follow through on.
- Work on implementing things incrementally, over many months, rather than all at once.
- Put them in your to do lists and calendars.
- Talk about them with the other people involved in your children's lives.

CONCLUSION

Parenting middle school children is daunting, but no matter how hard it gets, do not disengage. Do not be the hands-off parent. Do something today -- anything -- to connect with and guide your child. Then do it again tomorrow.

But be realistic about the fact that it is a long, messy process. You are training kids to become adults, and that is a long-term investment.

Parenting is an adventure of the greatest significance. It is your legacy.